Creation of the World
in /Xam mythology

JENI COUZYN

Creation of the World
in /Xam mythology

FIRELIZARD PRESS
2016

First People Artists at the Bethesda Arts Centre.
Back left to right: Gerald Mei, Rentia Davidson, Hilton Louw, Felicity Tromp,
Riaan Swiers, Merlyn Davidson, Esmerelda Tromp, Frendoline Malgas,
Sereline Tromp, Naasley Swiers, Angi Hendricks, Yvonne Merrington.
Front left to right: Martin Lackay, Julia Malgas, Rosie Jacobs, Sandra
Swiers (lead artist).

Published by Firelizard Press, 2016
info@firelizardpress.com

Text copyright © Jeni Couzyn, 2016
Photographs copyright © Jeni Couzyn and the Bethesda Foundation, 2016
except where otherwise stated

ISBN 978-0-9535058-5-2

Designed by Libanus Press Ltd, Marlborough
Printed by Hampton Printing (Bristol) Ltd

Contents

For Barbara,
who made this work possible

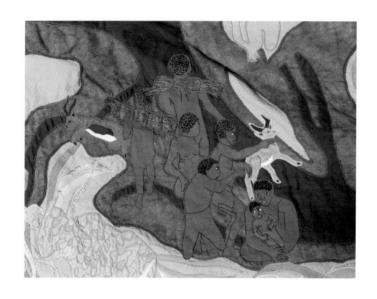

Preface

The stories explored by these narrative tapestries were recorded by linguists Wilhelm Bleek and Lucy Lloyd in Cape Town in the 19th century. The informants were /Xam Bushman prisoners, who had been released from prison to the custody of Wilhelm Bleek in order for him to continue his research into /Xam language and culture.

The main informant was ‖Kabbo (Dream). He was a shaman who understood that his people would very soon be extinct. He wanted his stories to be preserved for the future "by way of books" when there was no-one left to tell them. Now there is no-one left alive who speaks the /Xam language. The manuscripts exist in the Jagger library in Cape Town, in a collection of small handwritten notebooks. Many scholars have studied the manuscripts and made versions of the stories. The versions vary widely, as the notes are often incoherent and fragmentary.

The versions that follow were made by Jeni Couzyn, founder and artistic director of the First People Centre, Bethesda Arts Centre, Nieu Bethesda, Eastern Cape, South Africa. Couzyn, a South African by birth and education, Canadian and British citizen by adoption, is also a poet and psychotherapist. Couzyn consulted a wide selection of publications, and worked

from the original manuscripts. The poems that follow here include her own interpretations of the stories within a contemporary context.

The tapestries were made by Couzyn and the First People Artists at the Bethesda Arts Centre, working in a collaborative way developed by them. The artists are all people local to the Karoo village of Nieu Bethesda. They are of mixed descent, with a large Bushman genetic heritage clearly visible in their faces and bodies, and in remnants of their lost /Xam heritage. In their talent as artists, their knowledge and use of herbs, and in some fragments of hunter-gathering practices, their origins are still visible in their way of life. They identify themselves as /Xam, and are proud of their Bushman heritage, but have lost their language, and now speak Afrikaans.

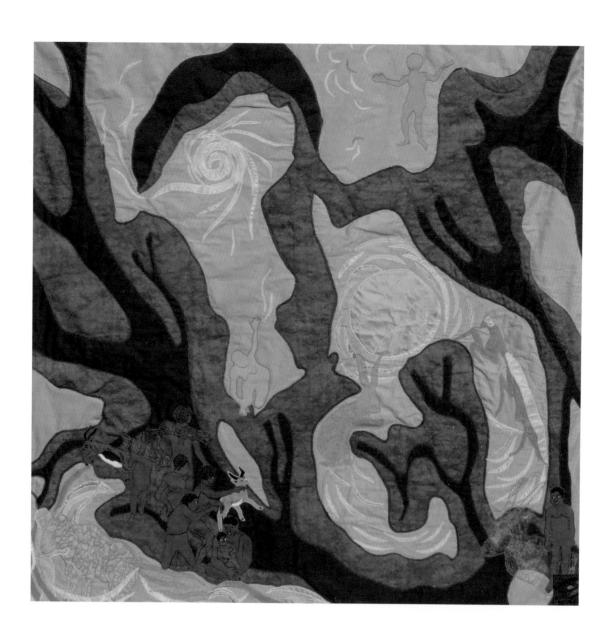

Introduction

These creation myths are from a vanished indigenous people who lived in peace and close to the natural world for thousands of years. As a culture the /Xam are extinct, and we have no way of knowing for sure what their myths might have meant to them. But for us the stories seem to be alive, relevant, and true – never quaint or charming – they are powerful and contemporary in their meanings.

They are much more than simple stories. They work at various levels, that could be broken down into four categories:

1. A simple story of children, parents, animals, and celestial bodies.
2. An intra-psychic description of the process of individual awakening.
3. A description of the evolution of humanity on earth.
4. An esoteric meaning, which is to do with the soul.

Myths are the stories that travel effortlessly across cultures and ages, connecting human beings with the wider collective psyche of humanity, and with nature. Their purpose is to explain our presence on earth. They work like dreams, creating meaning that resonates on many levels, as music does. Even in these desperate times, when our conscious connection to nature seems almost totally severed, myths are a living bridge to meaning.

At the Bethesda Arts Centre, we've explored the myths as dreams, complete in themselves, resonating in the collective consciousness of a species that has, collectively, become disconnected from our roots in the natural world. Myths in this situation become lights that can make the path a little clearer.

Lucy Lloyd, in the introduction to her wonderful *Specimens of Bushmen Folklore* in 1911, told a little story of her own experience of her /Xam informers' connection to nature "to show the living activity of Bushman beliefs." She'd picked a "splendid red fungus" in the woods and brought it home "in order to ascertain its name." A dedicated faithful worker and a benign scientist, Lloyd was simply doing her job, but the offended plant was now beginning to rot, and she asked |han‡kass'õ to throw it away. Shortly afterwards, "violent storms of wind and rain occurred". |han‡kass'õ had not thrown it away, but "put it down gently". It was, he explained to her, a "rain's thing" and the storms were a direct consequence of her asking him to *throw it away.*

Naming, a theme explored a lot in these stories, is about understanding nature and thereby getting power over it. This one vignette of thoughtless wastefulness is like a prophecy of all that was to come: modern man's obsessive attempts to dominate nature, our disrespect for the natural world, and in consequence, "very bad weather" (global warming, hurricanes, extremes of floods and drought). This theme is explored in the stories *Son of the Wind, First /Xam Man brings home a Young Lion,* and *The Origin of Death.*

In addition to their collective meaning, like most mythology these stories can also be understood as intra-psychic dramas. They are sophisticated descriptions of the on-going dramas that unfold in the individual psyche in its journey through a single human life. It is often at this level that these stories become most compelling. Most of us can recognise, for example, the conflict between that sluggish part of us that wants to remain unconscious, and the urgent need to "awake", (become more conscious) as in the *Creation of the Sun.*

The Origin of Death explores another intra-psychic conflict that most of us would acknowledge – a conflict between the rational mind that howls with rage and grief at the inevitable prospect of dying, or the death of a loved one, and that irrational, unnamed intelligence in us which sees all around it the cyclical quality of nature, and knows that there can be no death.

A third example of the stories as intra-psychic conflict is *The Son of the Wind.* Like the child in the story, the mind seeks to dominate that unnameable and untameable part of the psyche we sometimes call Soul by naming it. But the Soul, or the Spirit, or God, are mysteries the mind can't grasp or dominate, which is why so many religions say that God should not be named (Judaism) or give God a hundred names (Islam).

My background is poetry and psychoanalysis. Many books have been written about these stories. In particular I am grateful to Pippa Skotnes, who introduced me to these stories, and was herself a tireless "faithful worker" in her dedication to this archive. A number of poets have also made "versions" of the texts that read as contemporary poems. My offering has grown out of my love for the people of Nieu Bethesda with whom I work. I've lived with these myths at very close quarters for many years, as we cut out tiny pieces of material and sewed them together to bring them to life in colourful textile wall-hangings. My exploration springs from my love of meanings and symbols, and my familiarity with the stories as they took on concrete shapes and colours in the work of the First People artists.

A note on translation

In my versions, I've worked from the English texts published in *Specimens of Bushmen Folklore* (1911) and *Claim to the Country* (2007). I sensed constrictions on the narrators in their telling of the stories, imposed by the limited /Xam language of their scribes. Bleek and Lloyd were learning a foreign language as they worked. The /Xam narrators knew this, and I believe that they modified their choice of vocabulary to take this difficulty into account. I particularly notice a poverty of verbs, with endless repetition of simple verbs like spoke, walked, took, where it is quite clear from the context that yelled, sank, grabbed, would be more appropriate. So I've enriched the range of verbs where I sensed the need, relying on intuition to guide me. It felt a bit like trying to re-dye a piece of fabric that was stripped to shades of grey in the wash. What the original colours might have been when the story was told to /Xam listeners, we can only guess at. There must be many places where my narrative misses ‖Kabbo's and the other narrators' intended tone, and perhaps meaning, and for that I apologise to the /Xam storytellers, wherever they might be.

I've made no effort to condense the text to contemporary poetic standards of tightness, or enrich it with images or sounds I might use when writing ordinary poems. I've tried to capture the flow of the originals, keeping always in mind that these stories belong to an oral tradition. The rather rigid Victorian language of the original translations has a certain charm and authenticity, and I've kept that intact much of the time, sometimes retaining *thee* and *thou*, and only interspersing the odd contemporary colloquial phrase where I thought it necessary to bring the story to life.

The Creation of the Sun

In the early times, the sun was asleep in his house, shining for himself alone. The earth was cold and dark. The mothers couldn't dry the ant-larvae to eat so they were hungry, and the people were cold.

Then the old woman gathered the children together: "My children, creep up to that old man the sun while he is sleeping. Creep up to that old Sun Armpit, and fling him into the sky, so that the earth can be warm for us, so that all the world will be bright."

The Creation of the Sun

Narrated by ‖Kabbo 1871/3

This is the story I tell you.
At first the Sun was a sleeping man.
In his house on earth he gave forth brightness only
in the space around him.

The children were those who gently approached
to lift up the Sun-armpit while he lay sleeping.
The old woman was the one who inspired them.
Her head was white. The children listened,
while their mamma explained what the old woman said
and how to think about it.

They went to sit down, talked it over.
Younger brothers, older brothers,
companions spoke together.

They waited for him, that old man Sun.
They crept closer, stealthily approached him.
He lay eyes closed, meaning to stay asleep.

The old woman said to the children, 'O children going yonder!
You must speak to him when you throw him up,
instruct him. He must altogether become the Sun
that he may go forward, passing along in the sky.'

Stealthily they approached, looked at him, stood
perfectly still. Crept forward, stealthily reached him
grabbed him all together and lifted him up.
He was hot! They raised him, threw him up while he felt hot,
spoke to him, while he felt hot.

The children whispered 'O Sun! You must altogether stand fast,
you must go along, you must stand fast while you are hot.'
Then the children threw up that old man the Sun
while they felt that the old woman was the one speaking.

The old woman saw what they'd done.
The mothers saw, the husband saw.
He said, 'They've done it! Old Sun-armpit meant to stay asleep
but he's standing fast up yonder!'

The children came racing home. 'I took hold of him!'
'So did I!' The children felt themselves grow, felt like young men.
The youth called to his grandmother,
'O my grandmother we threw him up! I shouted like this:
Throw him up! Grasp the old man firmly! Throw up the old man!

We told him that he should altogether
become the Sun which is hot for we are cold.
We said: O my grandfather, Sun-armpit!
remain at that place, become the Sun which is hot
that the Bushman rice may dry for us, that you may make
the whole earth light,
that the whole earth may become warm in summer
that you may altogether make heat.

Therefore you must altogether shine,
taking away the darkness.
You must come. The darkness go away.'

THE CREATION OF THE SUN

This is a story about the awakening of consciousness. It is both a creation myth that describes the evolution of consciousness in life as we know it, and an intra-psychic account of the awakening of consciousness in the individual human being.

The story uses vivid imagery of the sleeping sun, in his house on the earth, to describe a state of unconsciousness. The sun is conceived as a forgetful old man, shining for himself alone. The image of sleep is an archetype for a pre-conscious state, as darkness is. Forgetfulness, in mystical tradition, is a metaphor for the state of unconsciousness where we are out of touch with that which enlightens us – so that all spiritual activity is an act of remembering. Light is an archetype for consciousness. Central to this vivid story is an old woman – archetype of wisdom, who acts as the agent for the process of transformation. She instructs the children through their mothers, on how to work with the sun. The story beautifully encapsulates the archetypal descent of wisdom through the mothers to their children, thus bringing change.

The old woman of the /Xam creation myth has good reason to want to jolt the sleeping sun into the sky. The people are cold, the world is dark and the ant chrysalides need to be dried for them to eat. In order to be alive, human beings need to be warm. We talk of the body being *cold*, meaning dead, and of the *cold* clay. The earth, in order for life to grow, also needs to be warm, and to be light. In the abstract, wisdom is "cold". The old woman feels cold. She explains in different ways, that the sun needs to be set on his path in the sky, so that the people can be "warm". At this level, the coming of consciousness, or the awakening of the sun in this account, is also the beginning of life on earth.

It's interesting to compare the story with the parallel account in the book of Genesis:

> In the beginning God created the heaven and the earth
> And the earth was without form, and void; and darkness was upon the
> face of the deep. And the Spirit of God moved upon the face of the waters.
> And God said, Let there be light: and there was light
> And God saw the light, that it was good: and God divided the light from
> the darkness.

The Judeo-Christian account has consciousness awakening spontaneously out of the Word. The /Xam account embodies God, or potential Consciousness, in a metaphor as a tired old man, sleeping in his house, and shining for himself alone. When he lifts his arm, light pours out from his armpit. His

awakening requires the intervention of two more agents: the old woman who is wise, and the children who are full of new life. The Old Woman is decisive in instructing the children how to surprise him into his necessary place in the sky, to light up the world, and to instruct him on the path he must follow in the sky. The mothers are important as intermediaries between the old woman, or Wisdom, and the children, who are the vital agents of transformation. Stealth, patience, mutual cooperation, and brave, decisive action are all necessary to accomplish the task.

||Kabbo, a Shaman and Rainmaker, told this story to Lucy Lloyd twice. In the second version, he gave more detail, describing the children as laughing, and having the old woman instruct them to hold in their laughter, and make sure that the younger children didn't laugh as they crept up on the sleeping sun. The laughing children represent the energy required for the transformation of wisdom, both cold, and in the dark, to the warmth of light and consciousness. Children are active and full of life. Laughter is their natural state. But they must go stealthily. This is an accurate description of the process of dawning consciousness, which comes with the subtlety of dreams, symbols, images, visions, flashes of insight, just like a group of tiptoeing, whispering children, holding in their mirth as they creep up on a sleeping old man, and hurl him into the sky. The old man is "cunning" – as contemporary psychoanalytic thinking reveals, the unconscious is rich in resources to trick the ego into remaining unconscious.

It is also necessary that the task of the Sun be spoken. The mystery of the spoken word has always engaged philosophers and mystics. The first word is seen to be the beginning in many traditions. In the version of the creation in John,1:1, "In the beginning was the Word, and the Word was with God, and the Word was God", the "Word" might mean pure idea. It is the Deity before creation. But not until the word is spoken, or the idea expressed in language, does creation begin to unfold. "And God said, Let there be light, and there was light." Speaking is crucial – the idea must be expressed for creation to begin its evolution. In the /Xam version, the old woman instructs the children to speak to the Sun as they throw him up into the sky, telling him that he must "altogether become the Sun", and what his work should be – lighting up the earth, making it warm, and drying the bushman rice so the people can eat.

In the /Xam story we feel the immediacy of the process of evolution. It has a sense of wholeness, including the old woman, the mothers, the children, and the old man Sun. Although it appears less abstract than the biblical account, it contains a paradox at its core as all creation myths do – there could not have been people before the creation of life on earth. Mystical ideas can only be explained in paradoxes. To understand we have to transcend to another level, where time is not linear, and the whole of creation, including the beginning and the ending, is continuously present.

Time like a pond, contains all life, and like pond-skaters we flit across it in little straight lines, imagining we are experiencing, in our brief linear histories, time itself. This story does not happen in linear time. It is continuous, with each conscious thought, and each breath of creation. The vault of the sky into which the sleeping sun is thrown is the vault of the skull.

The old woman, the mothers, children, and old man Sun, are both real and not real. They are splinters of the infinite Deity, representing pure idea. The story is woven with paradoxes, as mystical knowledge always is. At first the Sun is like us, an ordinary sleeping man. He is old and selfish (shining for himself alone). He is not open to others, or to the new. We have glimpses of what he potentially is when he raises his arm, and light pours from his armpit. But it is only when he is thrown up into the sky, at a great distance from us on the earth, that he becomes what he really is – the Sun, giver of light and warmth, sustainer of all life on earth. In so far as this is an intra-psychic story, there is a part of us like an old man, self-centred and closed to new ideas. It is only when we are awakened by the wisdom and laughter of that part of us that is wise, and full of new life, that we become conscious. In the greater scheme of the collective, it is only when life is awoken, that it transforms from ideas in the cold and half darkness, to a solar system spinning with planets, and the great cauldron of light and heat which is consciousness at the centre of being.

It is by reflection that we evolve. We are reflected in the stories we tell. Our unconsciousness is reflected in the sleeping Sun, living amongst us as an ordinary old man. When he is distanced by being thrown up into the sky, we are able to see in him a reflection of consciousness within ourselves. It is our own wisdom combined with our potential for change and our active life-energy that enables us to bring about this evolution.

In the /Xam account there are a number of references to the Sun's armpit. The children even address him as "armpit". ||Kabbo, in some additional notes, explains how the Sun was one of the First Bushmen, who were those who first inhabited the earth, and their children were those who worked with the Sun:

As his shining had been confined to a certain space at, and round his own dwelling, the rest of the country seemed as if the sky were very cloudy, as it looks now, when the Sun is behind thick clouds. [A description reminiscent of the "Cloud of Unknowing" and "the mists of forgetfulness".] The sky was black (dark?). The shining came from one of the Sun's armpits, as he lay with one arm lifted up. When he put down his arm, darkness fell everywhere; when he lifted it up again, it was as if day came.

My understanding of this image is that it expresses a complex idea to do with positive and negative space. The positive sun, as the positive space of a sphere, is a giant force too vast, dangerous and powerful for us even to approach with our eyes. Traditionally it is said that if we were able to look directly at God, we would be instantly blinded and burned to ash.

The armpit is a negative space, concave, hidden, and only a small part of the being as a whole. But it contains the unmistakable scent by which the whole can be reliably identified. "Anointing with sweat" is a practice used several times in this collection for indelibly fixing identity. By thinking of the Sun as "Sun's armpit", the dangerous concept becomes manageable as something one can relate to, albeit with great caution, stealth, and care. In the same way we are given an experience of God through prophets and mediators, as the direct experience would burn us to ashes. We're given a vivid picture of flashes of light, or consciousness in the dark, as the sun raises his arm, and light pours out from his armpit, and then as he drops his arm again, darkness descending. The sleeping sun is a vast cauldron of hidden light, momentarily revealed while he is on earth in a safe and very limited way – from his armpit when he raises his arm – until he is safely bestowed at a great distance on his correct path in the sky.

It is interesting that in the Christian structure, we are only able to experience God directly when he descends in the form of a man. In this story, it is the ascent from a sleeping man on earth to a giant light in the sky that makes

enlightenment (or consciousness) available as a source of life to benefit humanity.

The children need to use stealth and caution and daring to be successful in their task. They wait, they look, they approach with stealth. Taking the story as an intra-psychic drama, this is a vivid image of how inspiration works. The thought-forms are quick and elusive. They wait, they are hidden, they spring suddenly, decisively, into consciousness. And often the thought forms come in clusters, exactly like this cluster of eager children.

It is difficult to think of the sun without thinking of the moon, its reflection, or of the moon without the sun, its source of light. Reflection is one of the mysteries on which all mystical understanding of creation is founded. In these stories the sun and moon, reflector and reflection, weave together in a complex, cyclical way. Sometimes the moon is feminine, sometimes masculine. The old man sun cannot be separated from the wise old woman and active children who are necessary for him to become "altogether the sun". When the moon wanes it pleads with the sun to "leave for the children the backbone" – that sliver of light that transforms and grows into the new moon. In the reflection of the sun comes the waning of light, and then the renewal. There is a tradition that God created humanity so that he could see himself. All of nature works on reflection. All that we can ever know about ourselves is what we see reflected, in others, in our actions, or in our thoughts, and in the natural world.

In the story of the awakening of the Sun, the children speak the Sun to life in its role as Sun in the sky. Once awakened, and established on its path, it begins piercing and slicing the moon. The moon in its decline, begs the Sun to leave for the children "the backbone" – the sliver of light visible at the nadir of its waning. From its backbone, the moon itself grows full again, into a living being, a huge light in the sky so that people can "see their way at night". In the next story the moon is equal to the Sun in its importance in creation. The moon represents the light in the unconscious, where we see our way darkly. And it is here, in our confrontation with the moon, that we encounter death. Here also we encounter the idea of life renewing itself, again and again as we see the moon wax and wane, and wax again.

Sun Pierces the Moon with his Knife

This is how it happens: The sun comes, the day breaks, the darkness goes away. The sun sets, the darkness comes out, the moon rises. Moon brightens the darkness, taking away the darkness. The darkness departs.

Moon goes along, brightening the darkness. Moon sets. Sun is following close behind. Sun slices at Moon with his knife, each daybreak, a little more. Painfully Moon goes along, decaying away. He cries out to Sun, *O Sun! leave for my children the backbone!* Sun hears, and leaves alive for the children the backbone of the moon. A sliver. Painfully Moon goes home to become a new moon. He puts on a new stomach. He's alive! He becomes large, he becomes whole. And so it goes on.

Sun Pierces the Moon with his Knife

Narrated by ‖Kabbo 1871/3

Sun comes, darkness goes away, sun sets,
darkness comes, moon comes at night, day breaks,
sun comes out, darkness goes away, sun comes,

moon comes out, moon brightens the darkness, darkness departs,
moon comes out, moon shines, taking away darkness,
moon goes along, it's made bright the darkness, it sets,

sun comes out, sun follows the darkness,
sun takes away moon, moon stands, the sun pierces
moon with his knife.

Therefore moon decays away, therefore it cries
'*O Sun! leave for the children the backbone!*' Sun hears the moon's cry,
leaves moon's backbone, moon painfully goes away,

painfully returns home while he painfully goes along,
painfully returns home to become another moon which is whole,
again lives while he feels that he had seemed to die.

He becomes a new moon, he puts on a new stomach,
becomes large, feels alive. He comes, he is large, he's alive.
He feels that he is whole.

He goes along at night he's the moon that goes by night,
he is a shoe, that walks in the night he is shoe of the Mantis
walking by night lighting up the darkness.

The sun is here, all the earth is bright! The sun is here,
people walk in the light, perceive the bushes, see other people,
see their meat, see the springbok.

They head the springbok in summer, head the ostrich in summer,
shoot the springbok in summer, feel the sun on their bodies,
steal up to the gemsbok, steal up to the kudu.

They feel the sun shining, feel the whole place bright,
they visit each other while the earth is bright,
all is well. The sun shines upon their path.

In its rising the sun cuts pieces off the moon. The moon suffers and pleads with the sun till there is nothing left of him but the backbone. In other stories, such as *The Origin of Death* the moon is serene and wise, knowing that whatever death it suffers (not an "altogether death") it will return again alive. But in this story the pain of the moon is violent. It involves suffering we can all identify in our own lives – feelings of loss, feeling diminished, sometimes till all we valued is gone. Usually we experience loss, as the moon does in this story, as pain. The moon becomes a pitiful old man, hobbling away, nothing left of him but the backbone.

The body parts in this myth are powerful metaphors for inner states. Like all good images they work well at a concrete level, as well as functioning as indicators of a deeper meaning. The crescent sliver of the waning moon can easily be visualised as the backbone of a bent old man. The backbone of a person is that essential core that carries all the nerves from the body to the brain. It represents the essential channel of the life-force through which the person functions. It also relates to our core-self at an emotional level. In our language we talk of a weak-willed person as *"having no back-bone"* or *"spineless"*. We talk of *"back-breaking work"* and *"the straw that broke the camel's back"*. In this encounter, the sun could demolish the moon utterly, but instead he "hears the moon's cry" and "leaves for the children [new life] the backbone". The moon loses all but his essential life, and his will to live. Similarly the metaphoric use of "stomach" works at both levels. The new roundness of the waxing moon can easily be compared with a large stomach and it has strong contemporary echoes in our language. We say *"I have no stomach for that"*, or if confronting some deception or cruelty, *"it turned my stomach"*. To "put on a new stomach" is to find a resolute part of ourselves able to face grave difficulties and carry on. The point of the story is that the moon does not remain diminished. He returns to fullness and to wholeness.

At a metaphysical level this story is about reflection. The moon reflects the light of the Sun. In itself, it has no light. It inhabits darkness. Yet in reflecting the light of the sun, the moon shines with great beauty.

We are that.

The Sun is the Divine light. We as humans are reflections of that Divine light. We live as the moon does, in a cycle of waxing and waning. We are hacked down, we suffer, we wane, we limp home. Then gradually we begin to recover. Gradually we "put on a new stomach" and grow until we feel whole again, and the cycle begins again.

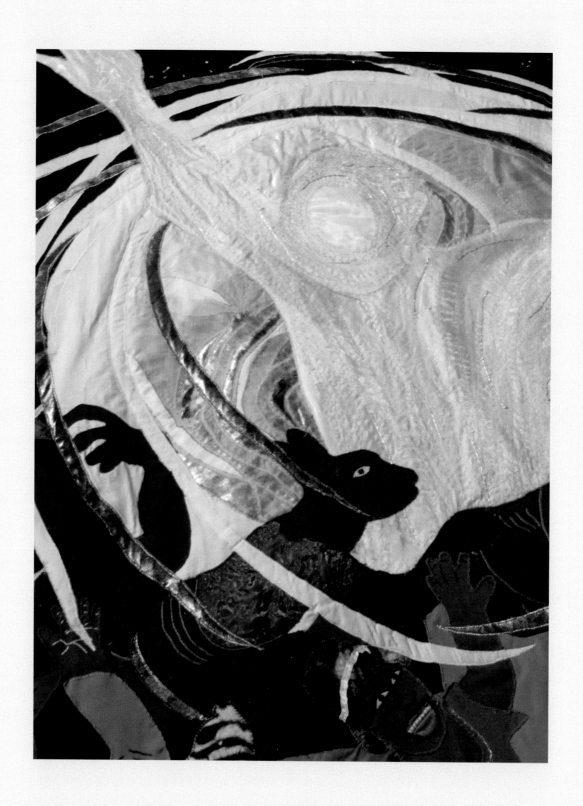

The Origin of Death

In the early time there was no death. Hare was crying: *My mother is dead. She will not come again!*

Moon was firm: *Hare, your mother has died, but she will, like me, like all of nature, return alive.*

Oh no no no, cried Hare. *My mother is altogether dead. She will not living return.* He cried and howled. There was no stopping him.

Moon became angry and cleft his mouth. He cursed the Hare: *From now on you, and all humanity, will die, and when you have died, not living return.*

The Origin of Death

Narrated by Diä!kwãin, 1875

Our mothers have told us, it was the hare who cried,
would not be silent when his mother died.
The moon explained:

Your mother being dead will again return alive.
The people should be like me, and do what I do.
When I am dead, I again living return.

The hare spoke. There was no stopping him.
'My mother is altogether dead! She will not again living return.
Therefore I will cry greatly for my mother!'

He howled for his mother. He moaned, he yelled
and lamented. The moon became angry and cleft his mouth.
He cursed the hare:

This person shall become altogether a hare,
and he shall always bear a scar on his mouth.
The dogs will chase him, and tear him to pieces,

And he will altogether die.
And they who are men,
they shall altogether dying go away when they die.

Prayer to the Moon

Take my face yonder
Give me thy face
When thou hast died
Thou dost again living return
When we did not perceive thee
Thou dost again lying down come
That I may also resemble thee
For the joy yonder
Thou dost living return.

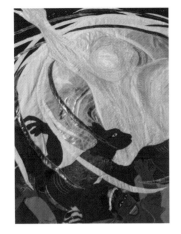

The moon and the hare have long been associated in mythology all over the world, along with mythic stories of death, resurrection, and immortality. In one story widely found in African mythology, the hare is sent by the moon to give the gift of immortality to mankind, but gets it wrong, and instead bestows mortality and brings death to the human world.

The /Xam story told here is probably a much earlier version, deeper in meaning. The hare in this story is not just foolish and negligent – he is a much more rounded character, grieving for his mother and indulging in his grief in a way that prevents him from seeing and hearing the truth of the moon's message. He is so busy howling about his mother's death that he is deaf to the moon's words, and that which is before his eyes – the cyclical waning and waxing of the moon. He chooses to cling to his grief, and obstinately refuses to be moved by the comfort he is being offered. The moon says: "I said to him about it, that they (the people) should also be like me; that which I do; that I, when I am dead, I again living return. He contradicted me, when I had told him about it."

The moon intended to give human beings joy. He explained that death was a sleep, from which we would again wake. He invited the hare to be like him, and see how he always returned. The moon expected to be heard by the hare. He expected the hare to say: "Yes, my mother lies sleeping. She will presently arise." The moon does not say, in these stories, that dying is not painful. He goes painfully home with each death, he painfully goes away in his waning, but then he returns and grows again to his full brightness. The metaphor of sleep is one we can easily understand, experiencing, each night, a little death, where all our senses are lost. And then in the morning awaking refreshed, and everything begins again.

This story probes the central paradox that we as human beings have to grapple with all our conscious lives – the mind, able to conceive of immortality, confronting its own death. Civilizations transcend this difficulty in different ways – primarily with religious beliefs. For the /Xam, when a person dies, they become a star – distant, eternal – a point of light in the vast canopy of stars that enfolds us when the moon wanes. When the /Xam inhabited central South Africa, they would have lived nightly under the brilliance of the thick blanket of stars still visible on clear nights over the Karoo. There is a sense of stillness and completion in this profoundly comforting image. It suggests peace, and acceptance. Unlike many traditions, it does not imply any linear evolution of the soul after death, but it does place the human spirit firmly in the realm of the immortal, among the celestial lights.

The moon/hare story, on the other hand, treats mortality as a terrible and violent punishment for a wrong attitude in life. I have come to see this story as an intra, rather than an inter-psychic account of the consequences of such an attitude. The moon represents that part of the psyche that knows itself to be part of nature. It is the "higher self" as described by Jung, or the "soul". The hare represents the "little self" – the ego, or the swift and doubting mind, who "springs away, and doubling comes back".

The story is powerfully contemporary in its message. When man/woman-kind separates itself from the natural world, it separates itself from the rhythm of life – the natural cycle of life ebbing and flowing like breath – and being renewed on an eternal basis. This is the order of life visible around us in all nature. By declaring itself separate, man/womankind becomes victim to the merciless hounds of thought who will tear it to pieces. We will forever lie on bare ground, defenceless as the hare without sheltering bushes, and we will speak with split lip, unable to utter wholeness.

The moon is an accurate image for the tides of human lives, and for the waxing and waning of a human life in its entirety. Like the new moon we start as a sliver, grow, reach our full potential, and then at a certain point, begin to wane again, till like babies we are without continence, power, mind, strength – loss after loss, each painful, till we are again a sliver of our former glory.

In this story, as in other mythologies, mortality is inflicted as a deep wound. It keeps the "hare" part of the mind in a victim state, forever vulnerable. In the Greek myths, the immortal Gods look down at mortal humanity from a great height, vacillating between contempt and pity. In the biblical version, there is the banishment from paradise – analysed, in contemporary interpretations, as a necessary evolution from innocence. But there's no possible ambiguity in this Origin of Death story. Here the punishment is a terrible curse, to sleep on bare ground without sheltering bushes, be plagued by vermin and hunted by hounds. The punishment is for obstinacy and self-pity. The "hare" part of the psyche has set himself up as a diva, howling at the centre of a narcissistic drama that cuts him off from nature, of which he is part. We separate ourselves from nature at our gravest peril.

Humanity is left with a prayer to the moon – a prayer to become like the moon, immortal. There is no assurance, no answer, no going back. The curse is absolute and irrevocable. The only antidote is that we live in a state of harmony with nature, knowing ourselves to be part of it.

As I write this, a Syringa tree is in full bloom outside my door in the courtyard, reminding me of the poignancy of this aspect of nature. And I am waiting, with my friends who have come here to teach art, for the moon to wane so that we can see the Karoo stars in their full glory – a sight not very different from that which the /Xam narrators might have seen from their small fires in the vast Karoo darkness thousands of years ago.

THOUGHTS ON THE ORIGIN OF DEATH

What does it mean to become altogether a hare?

It means to be forever pursued by dogs. It means to be forever pursued by terrors, a victim of fear, unarmed, and helpless. It means to be incapable of inner contemplation, unable to think and consider calmly, unable to connect with the cyclical quality of nature of which we are part. It means to be always at the mercy of predators who have no mercy.

Who are the dogs who pursue the hare? They are the terrors that keep us victims. Fear of losing what we have, fear of not getting what we want, fear of the unknown, fear of death. To be pursued by dogs is to live in perpetual danger and terror. To be torn to pieces by them is to lose that cohesive identity we call "I", a sense of wholeness we identify as being ourselves.

What does it mean to "altogether die and not living return?" It is only in our inability to identify with the moon, learn from it, *be* it, that we become mortal. In so far as we are able to connect with the cyclical quality of nature, we are able to experience and trust our own immortality.

What does it mean to have a cleft mouth? I think this is to do with how we are able to express ourselves. Our expression, with a cleft mouth, will always be distorted. It will contain the garbled quality of psychic damage. Unlike the pure voices of the rest of nature, our voice will be full of lies and deception.

The Girl who Made Stars

A girl of the early times was hungry and cross in her confinement hut during her first menses. She was not allowed to gather food for herself, and had to rely on the !huin roots her mother brought her. Nor was she allowed to be seen by the young hunters, or eat their meat, in case their arrows should grow cold and their hunting fail.

The pressure inside her grew and grew till she flung the wood ashes from her fire into the sky. "You who are wood ashes, you will altogether become the Milky Way, and sail through the sky, following your footprints, so people coming home by night can see their way."

The girl who made stars gazed at the night sky and was full of wonder. Power came through her as she thought about new life being created in her body, and the stars treading their path through the sky as they should.

She saw how the sky lay still, but the stars were the ones who moved, sailing along their path. Darkness comes out, darkness is upon the ground. The stars, at first white, wax red. They feel that turning, they follow the sun. The !huin roots are stars. The people are stars. The Milky Way gently glows, lighting up the ground.

The Girl who Made Stars

Narrated by ‖Kabbo, who got it from his mother, !kwi-an

The girl arose, plunged her hands into the wood ashes,
threw the wood ashes into the sky. She told the wood ashes:
'You must altogether become the Milky Way.

You must white lie along in the sky.
The Milky Way must go round with the stars,
it must lie as it should while the stars sail along.

When the sun goes back, the stars shall go to fetch the daybreak,
they shall sail along following their footprints.
The Milky Way lying comes to its place to descend as it should.

It goes round with the stars. They turning pass over the sky
while the sky lies still. They set, they come out,
they follow their footprints. When the sun strides out

they become white, when it sets darkness closes in,
they wax red. Turning, the stars follow the sun. They feel the night.
They feel their brightness.

The Milky Way gently glows lighting the ground.
Everything is changed.
The people can return home by night.'

The Milky Way feels itself wood ashes as it glows in the sky.
It feels the magnificent girl who spoke it into being
to light the people by night.

Her eyes turn the springbok wild.
This girl-creator waiting for her blood to come
confined in her hut flaring at her mother, tossing !huin roots into the sky.

Arrowheads turn to ice at her touch, her father alone
can give her meat. Her glance is feared by the bravest hunters
even her saliva a thing of power.

THE GIRL WHO MADE STARS

Like so many of the /Xam stories we have explored in our work at the Bethesda Arts Centre, in this story the feminine energy is dominant in the creation of the cosmos. Here, a girl menstruating for the first time, throws wood ash and edible roots into the sky, so that they can become stars, and light the people's path as they walk by night. With wonderful directness and clarity, this myth locates the creator of the Milky Way and all the stars in the dawning womanhood of a pubescent girl.

It reminds me of another story, told in the context of Native American culture, called *Daughters of Copper Woman* which describes how young menstruating women are separated from the tribe during their "sacred" time, when they are highly sensitive, somewhat unpredictable, and above all immensely creative. The young woman of this story represents an archetype of fertility. She is hungry, quick-tempered, passionate, and visionary. Her creative act throws the stars into the sky. Creation is a continuous present, not a fixed event in linear time. An ordinary young life on the brink of fertility as a vessel for this immense act of creation, is a just image.

In an additional explanation, ‖Kabbo tells Lucy Lloyd that she was angry with her mother for not giving her enough !huin roots to eat. She was confined during this time to a very small hut, and somewhat feared, as her eating the young men's game could destroy their ability as hunters, and a look from her could turn the springbok wild. She may be a fragile girl, but she is powerful and therefore feared. She knows how the Milky Way should turn in the sky, she knows how the stars should sail along in the sky, "following their footprints". And she knows how they should follow the sun, becoming white when the sun rises. But she is also benign. It is in order that the people should be able to see by night that she creates the stars.

As in both of the previous stories, an essential part of the creation is the spoken word. The girl instructs the stars and the Milky Way, speaking them into being. She instructs the wood ash on how to become the stars, and throwing, speaks them into being, in much the same way as the children of the first story, throwing, speak the sun into the sky. She also throws up edible roots – as if the creation is coming from within the earth itself. It is a form of expression, from within to without, made in full consciousness with the act of speaking. It reminds me of John's description of creation in the New Testament: "In the beginning was the Word, and the Word was with God, and the Word was God." This idea also turns up in psychoanalytic thought, where the infant is said first to be conceived in the minds of the parents, and later in flesh.

Bleek includes a note added by ||Kabbo, that this person of the early race, was the first girl. He adds that she is thought to have acted ill, and was finally shot by her husband. He goes on that "These [early race people] are said to have been stupid, and not to have understood things well." My own understanding of what he meant was that the man who became her husband, and the others of her community, thought she had acted ill, behaved stupidly towards her, and did not understand her power. It seems that she suffered the fate of women throughout history who are too powerful.

45

The Woman and the Rainbull

During her menses, the young /Xam woman must remain in her hut, away from others. In this strangely beautiful and moving story, while the young woman is lying on her mat, the Rainbull picks up her scent, and is attracted towards her. She too, is attracted by his scent. They meet, and she rubs buchu on his forehead to calm him. Then she mounts him in a tender yet frightening meeting and he carries her away. Later she escapes from him through the trees. If she had remained, he might have drowned her in his water pit, where she would be turned into a frog. The older women burn horns when she returns, to stop him being angry.

The Woman and the Rainbull

Narrated in 1878 by |han‡kass'õ, who heard it from his mother, |Xabbi-an

Long ago a young woman was courted by the Rain.
She was lying in her menstruating hut
her child beside her on the kaross, when

Rain scented her and the place became misty.
Drawn by her scent, trotting he came in search of her.
He came rising out from his water-pit home, leaving it dry.

He came courting, misty and damp and potent
and as he came she scented his fragrance
scented his breath, the whole place fragrant with him.

'Who can this man be, who comes to me smelling so sweet?'
He was so close, crouching at the entrance.
She watched him, overcome with his sweet scent.

She took up buchu and rubbed it on his forehead
to calm him. He was too eager – she pushed him away
and tied on her kaross.

Carefully she laid down her child, covered it with a skin,
then mounted him, mounted the Rain –
and he carried her away.

She thought she would go go go go she thought she would not live
she thought she'd be carried to the Rainbull's water-pit
whence he courting came, and become a frog.

When did she start looking at the trees, thinking of home?
'Set me down at that big tree, for I ache.
Go close to the trunk, under the branches.'

Under the tree she stroked his neck
she calmed him with buchu till he fell asleep. She climbed
up off his back and stole softly upward through the branches.

The Rainbull arose from his sleep and returned to the spring
whence he'd courting come, believing the woman
was still on his back, sank down down down into the water

while she went along greening. She was the wise one
protecting her people, handling the Rainbull as she should
responding to the Rain, aware of the danger.

In her hut, musky from their meeting, rank
with the scent of ‖khou, that Rain's thing
she burnt buchu, rubbed herself clean with buchu scent

and the old women burned horns to appease his anger.

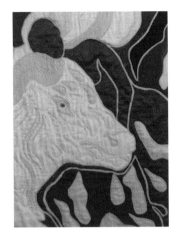

This story wonderfully makes the connection between land and sky. As in the previous story, it centres around the young woman and fertility. Here, it concerns a union between the earth, represented by a young woman, and the rain in the form of a bull. If the young woman can negotiate the necessary dangers of her love affair with him, they will green the earth. To wrench the frightening power of water and the delicate thirst of earth into a love affair between a woman and a bull is something only mythology could do.

At an intra-psychic level, the Rainbull is the instinctual aspect of the psyche, wild, creative and dangerous, while the young woman is the considering, mindful aspect, concerned with preserving life. Through their mutual attraction and safe union, the creativity of the individual is maintained.

The bull is an archetypal symbol of fertility, the animal embodying the mightiest procreative power of all animals. It is also extremely dangerous, as procreation itself is. In this story a young woman is alone with her baby in the menstruating hut when the Rainbull catches her scent. She too catches his scent in the scent of the rain, and is attracted. Theirs is a complex love affair, fraught with danger, and with a huge imbalance of power. His massive muscular body could crush her in a second. Carefully, she prepares buchu to sedate him. Then she mounts him, and he carries her off on his back. She's in great peril, because if unchecked, he'll drown her in his water-pit whence he came, or even worse, turn her into a frog. When the time is right, she sedates him again, climbs off his back onto a tree without his noticing, and "green", creeps safely home. (After rain, the green of leaves creeps up into the trees.)

For the /Xam, who lived in fragile bush shelters, good rain was gentle rain. Fierce rain, thunder and lightning, sudden downpours, and flash floods, can be massively destructive. So the union has to be intelligent and wise. In order to prevent the Rainbull returning and causing damage when the woman returns home alone, the old women burn horn. Horn is often a symbol of male potency, and the burned horn appears to be a way for the women to secure control over the energy which unchecked could destroy them.

In this story, women who have been captured by the Rainbull are turned into frogs – often associated with transformation in myths and legends. Because they begin life as tadpoles, mature as great leapers with powerful legs, and then, as amphibians inhabit both elements of water and land, they are seen to be transitional between heaven and earth, or different planes of existence before and after physical death. A further ambiguity is the location of the Rainbull himself. Although rain comes down from the sky, his home is below the water, which is below the earth. He doesn't fall from above, he rises up from below.

Male sexuality is necessary for procreation, but dangerous if allowed to rampage unchecked. Rape, bullying, brutal overpowering of women by men is an ever-present threat. The energy, like thunderstorms damaging the earth, needs to be managed with caution. The wisdom of this story is as recognisable for the contemporary First People artists at the Centre, as it is for women and men all over the world, now, exactly as it was tens of thousands of years ago.

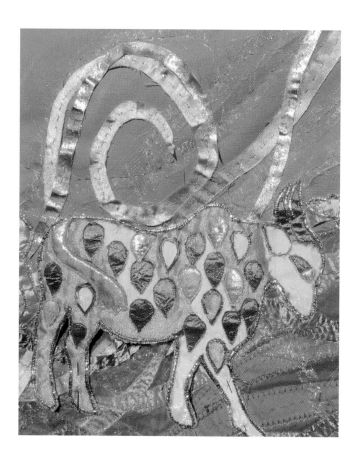

This story was told to Lucy Lloyd, a single Victorian woman, by ǀhanǂkass'õ, described as a lively and talented story teller who used many hand gestures in his narrations. She seems to have got into some difficulty with the sexual material, for example, "And the young woman became aware of him, as he came up; while he lowered his tail (?)". She doesn't attempt to explore in any further notes what "lowering his tail" might have meant, leaving the question mark to speak for itself of her discomfort. Between the lines there is rampant lust, desire, and sensuality, not only in the Rainbull, but in the young woman as well. The energy that binds heaven and earth is desire.

The Son of the Wind

In the early times, a boy is playing ball with the son of the wind. "There it goes, Na-ka-ti, there it goes!" calls the son of the wind, as he rolls the ball to Na-ka-ti. "There it goes, Comrade" calls Na-ka-ti, for he doesn't know the name of his companion.

Na-ka-ti goes to his mother. "Tell me the name of my companion, so I can also call out his name when I roll the ball." His mother says, "You must not utter the name of the Son of the Wind, till father shelters the hut strongly, and then you must scamper home, or the wind will blow you away."

But Na-ka-ti goes on begging his mother to tell him so eventually she gives in: "Ierriten-!kuan-!kua it is; !gau-!gaubu-ti it is." When his father has finished sheltering the hut, Na-ka-ti calls out to his friend, as he rolls the ball: "There it goes, /erriten-!kuan-!kuan, there it goes, !gau-!gaubu-ti".

The son of the wind lies down on the ground and blows till the dust rises. He kicks violently on the ground till the people's eyes are red and stinging, and all the huts and all the shelters of the people are blown away. At last the wind's mother comes out and raises her son from the ground and calms him until he is still. And then the wind is still.

56

The Son of the Wind

Narrated by ǀhanǂkass'õ, 1878, who heard it from his mother, ǀxabbi-an.

Na-ka-ti rolled a ball with his comrade, son of the wind.
'There it goes, O Na-ka-ti! There it goes!' exclaimed son of the wind.
'O comrade! There it goes!' replied Na-ka-ti

but he wasn't happy. He wanted more than being a boy.
He wanted power. He wanted to call his comrade by name.
'Our Mother' said Na-ka-ti, 'tell me comrade's name.'

'I will not. You must at first be silent.
Wait till father shelters for us the hut – shelters it strongly.
Then I will tell you comrade's name.

When I speak for you that name
you must dash for home, scamper into the hut to be safe
for you'll feel that the wind would blow you away.'

She knew this, the wise /Xam woman, who speaks rarely,
the mother of the boy who is always there at her skirt strings,
always rolling a ball, always wanting something.

Na-ka-ti went again to roll the ball but back he came
nagging at her, 'Our mother, tell me, tell me comrade's name.'
She exclaimed 'Erriten-kuan-kuan it is, Gau-gaubu-ti it is!'

Why did she tell him the name that should not be spoken?

At first, Na-ka-ti obeyed his mother and was silent
even when the other called out his name.
They rolled the ball, two children playing together.

He watched his father sheltering the hut with a screen of bushes
but he was growing more impatient by the minute
wishing his father would finish.

When his father at last sat down, Na-ka-ti shouted
'Ereiten-kuan-kuan, there it goes! O Gau-gaubu-ti, there it goes!
There it goes O Gau-gaubu-ti!' He felt like a god.

The son of the wind leaned over, slowly he fell down,
he lay down, kicking violently upon the vlei,
the bushes were smashed, the shelters were broken, the huts vanished.

The dust rose up, rose up, rose up.
People were blinded with dust
and could see nothing.

Then mother of the wind came out of her hut. The world held its breath.
She grasped her son and raised him protesting onto his feet.
The noise of the wind was the creaking of his knees.

So he became still.

I wish that the wind would gently blow for us
so we could climb to the place behind the hill by the dry river bed where
the springbok are plentiful.

THE SON OF THE WIND

This is a story about a boy who attempts to place himself on equal terms with one of the elements of nature by trying to dominate the wind. But who can control the wind? The wind represents the breath that holds all of life together. The wind is "the breath of God". In some traditions, "the breath is the soul in the body". The breath we breathe out is transformed and made clean by the trees and plants of the earth. At every moment the breath we breathe in penetrates all the cells of our bodies. Through the breath we are woven into the tapestry of all living things.

The boy's reason for attempting this feat is ignorance and inflation. His friend calls out his name as they roll the ball to each other, and he can't respond on equal terms as he doesn't know the name of his companion. "There it goes, Na-ka-ti!" calls the wind, but Na-ka-ti wants to respond with status and authority.

At a superficial level the children playing presents a delightful scene – one we could easily imagine today where a child chases a ball as it is blown about by the wind, and for him the wind is a child like himself, a friend, imaginary or real. But in this story there is nothing imaginary about the son of the wind. He is real, and although he can play, like a child, he is also powerful, and uncontrollable. At an intra-psychic level, the son of the wind represents that part of us that we can never "know". We "play" with it, but we can never name it, or dominate it. As humans we have to live with the presence of the unknown within ourselves. This is the divine aspect of the human being. In sacred literature it is often associated with the words "awe" and "the fear of God".

The /Xam lived closer to nature than we, in the 21st century, can easily imagine. They walked barefoot on the earth. Walking in the bush on a moonless night, without a torch, we can get a glimpse, but we can't hold it for long. They were part of the dark, part of the earth. But even for us, with our steel and cement and machines and electric lights, the wind in a rage, can devastate our cities in a few minutes, and frequently does. We are helpless to intervene, and can only dive for cover.

This story shows how the /Xam people lived in harmony with nature in a fully conscious way, and knew their place in relation to the natural world. The boy tries to dominate and rival the wind's power, and the consequences are serious for him and the tribe. The son of the wind becomes enraged, destroying the shelters of all the people, and blowing up the dust till their eyes are all burning. Only a superior power, the wind's mother, can calm him.

Power, in this story, is asserted through the magical process of naming.

In magic, ancient and modern throughout the world, naming is a way of controlling something or someone. In contemporary science, naming something, such as the atom, or neutrinos, or black holes, is the beginning of a power-interaction. Similarly in medicine, we begin the process of overcoming a disease by naming the agent that has caused it. In traditional belief systems of some indigenous peoples, the "true" name of a person must be kept secret, to protect them from enemies. In some religious traditions the name of God must never be spoken.

By calling out the name of the Son of the Wind, thus seeking equality with him, the child disturbs the natural order of the elements. The wind, like a furious toddler giant, strikes back by having a tantrum, and blowing away the huts and shelters of the child's family, and all the people.

This ancient cautionary tale could well have been written in contemporary times to address humanity's disconnection and lack of respect for the natural world, resulting in ecological disasters that threaten life on earth. In mythological time, time is not linear. It is an ever present whole, and what was true for the /Xam tens of thousands of years ago is equally true for us today. The wind story is a brilliant vehicle for this understanding of how we are connected with nature, because wind (breath) is both outside of us and within us, keeping us alive. The profound understanding the /Xam had of the natural world that emerges in these stories, confirms our human place in it, as delicate and lightly balanced as theirs was.

A TYPICAL WORKSHOP:
MAKING THE SON OF THE WIND

As always, the work began with talking. How is the way a child plays with the wind different from the way a grown-up might fear, or try to use the wind? What is the meaning of the story? What is the significance of knowing someone's name? What other names are secret? What is the power that knowing someone's name gives you?

We talked about how in some traditions the name of God should never be spoken. In the Jewish tradition God's name is a sacred secret. In the Islamic tradition, God has a hundred beautiful names. In North American Indian tradition, a young man finds out his true, hidden name during initiation, and that is kept secret as a totem of power. We talked about how in magic, naming things by their secret name gives the magician power over them. And about how in science, we seek to control the world around us by naming, and in that way, understanding it. We talked about the importance for parents in finding the right name for their child.

For us, the story of Son of the Wind came to mean this: At first humanity "plays" with nature, accepting that nature has great power. Then humanity gets greedy for power, and seeks to dominate nature. As in the story of the lion that follows, the wise woman, who in this case is the little boy's mother, warns him against the danger of seeking to dominate nature, but as in the lion story, her advice is ignored. When the child triumphantly calls out

the wind-boy's name, he has a tantrum and blows down the huts of the human beings. It is left to the feminine wisdom, his mother, to calm him down, and raise him up from the ground where he is having his tantrum.

We had loved the story of the son of the wind for a long time, but depicting the wind in images was daunting, and we had often thought about it, and then put it aside. When we got lottery money to make the tapestry, there was no more avoiding it. We began with a colour palette. We chose a dark maroon wine colour, but went with pale blues and silvers as a back-up, in case the deep reds didn't work. Very soon it became clear that the blues and silvers would be the way to go.

Then we invited all the children of the participating artists, along with their friends and cousins, to come to the centre and move on our stage. We asked them to imagine themselves as the wind, blowing about. Then we asked them to be themselves, blown about. Then working in twos, or small groups, we asked them to blow each other about.

The following day the grown-ups did the same thing. Then began the weeks of drawing and designing. Everyone drew pictures for the tapestry. People posed while others drew them. We tried lots of different poses. We made the sound of the wind. We lay down on the floor and had tantrums. We worked in twos, the tantrum wind-boy, and his mother calming him. We

leapt up on tables and desks being the human boy, triumphantly calling out the wind's name. Meanwhile people drew and drew. We covered kilometres of rough paper with charcoal marks, till the characters were in our bodies as well as on paper. Finally we chose a selection of drawings, and laid them out on huge sheets of paper on the floor.

We finished the tapestry at 1am on Saturday 29 May, 2011. The big push at the end was, as always, an intense time for everyone. In the final hours, people would push the iron from one to another as their exhausted arms ached too much to continue ironing. Martin made coffee and cake at five, when everyone should have been going home. Later he made supper. At midnight we made more coffee and cut up some fruit.

Making Son of the Wind changed something at the Bethesda Arts Centre. ‖Kabbo had wanted the stories he and his fellow prisoners told to float on the wind to future generations when the /Xam had ceased to be. During the process of making the Son of the Wind, we decided that the time had come to create a dedicated gallery at the Centre for our Myth tapestries, so that they could be kept on permanent display. The big studio was sealed from dust and sunlight, and transformed into our permanent gallery of /Xam mythology, open to all the world.

The First /Xam Man Brings Home
a Young Lion

A hunter finds a young lion, and brings it home, pretending to his wife that it is a dog his brother gave him, to help him in his hunting. But its eyes are yellow, its ears are short. His wife knows he is lying, and arms her children with fire-sticks. The young lion grows, and eventually, while hunting with its master, kills and eats him. The story ends with the wife and children having to move, as their home is now known to the lions, and too dangerous to live in.

The First /Xam Man Brings Home a Young Lion

Narrated by ||Kabbo, 1873

The First /Xam man found the lion's children.
He lifted up a little lion in his arms
and brought it home. His wife protested,

'What kind of dog is this? It looks nothing like a dog. Its head
looks different. Its ears are too short.' He coolly answered,
'My little brother gave me this puppy.

He thought I should feed it and bring it up.'
She burst out: 'This is a young lion you've brought home!'
—'Don't insult my brother's dog!'

He was lying. 'This thing is a lion cub!
Its head's too big, its feet are nothing like a dog's paws.
Its coat is red.' He knew she knew, but he insisted:

'It's a puppy! The eldest of the litter,
which is why it looks as it does.'
His wife whispered to the children, and they listened.

He coaxed her, 'Feed this puppy nicely for us. We need
gemsbok children. He could with his speed catch for us
gemsbok children, so we could eat flesh.'

But his wife understood danger.
'The lioness will follow your spoor to our house
for you've brought a lion cub into our home.'

She placated him to gain time. 'Set down your dog, go and fetch wood
so we can sleep beside a fire.' When he was gone, she urgently
gathered her children. She had to make them understand.

'Is your father near?' 'He's collecting wood.' Is he listening?' 'No.'
'Watch him and tell me when he comes near. I must talk to you.'
'I'm watching. You can talk to me.' Her eldest boy, her treasure.

'Listen. You don't quite believe me, when I tell you
that this thing's a young lion. Look at the shape of its head.
Look at its big yellow eyes.'

The young lion stared icily at her. 'See how it stares at me
when I speak its name.' The young lion looked around.
'You'll be terrified, when you're out with your father. He's deceived us.

Look at its huge mouth. I told your father to keep it away from us,
to tie it up if he thinks it's a dog. But I never saw a dog like this
with a head like this lion's head.'

The lioness, from afar, roared, calling her little son.
The lion cub raised its head, listening. The woman pinched her child,
hissed in his ear: 'This thing is alien to us.'

'I'm scared, now I see' – his voice a whisper.
'That voice you hear, it's the cub's mother, calling to her son.
Do you imagine the lion would choose to live with us?

Your father's deceived us – he's a crazy man
to bring a lion into his home. The mother lioness, seeking her son
will come and find us. Soon.'

The child shivered. She kept on. 'When your father has reared it …
but still you don't quite believe me!' 'I do. You speak true, my mother.
A thing of the night is the thing that is here.'

'It's alien. A dog's feet are white and smooth, a lion's feet are hairy.
A lion's ears are black on the back, and rounded, not pointy like a dog's ears.
This is a thing whose parents are man-eaters.

It knows itself to be Lion, a thing of the night.
It listens to its mother far off, and remembers her voice from long ago.
It hears her calling, seeking to find it.'

'Oh my husband,' cried the woman,
'Why did you bring us a young lion?' He wouldn't budge:
'This is a dog my little brother gave me.

I asked him for it. Why do you glare at it like this?
You're not looking properly. Look closely – you'll see clearly
it's my little brother's dog. Its father looks exactly the same.

It's a fine male pup.'
She said, 'That sweet pup is a dog of your dreams. This one's vicious.
I'm so much afraid.' But he plunged on:

'It looks exactly like its dam.
My little brother will bring her with him when he comes here
so you'll see for yourself. He told me that this pup's mother kills gemsbok.'

'You're lying! You want to convince me it's a dog,
but it'll kill me. Its mother in the bush roars for her cub with a lion's voice.
I've known that voice since I was a child living with my parents.

It's a little lion, and nothing can change that.'
'Nag, nag, nag. You accuse me of dreaming up a dog – falsely.
I asked for this dog, so we could own a dog of our own.

Well, I'll take it hunting, and it'll catch a young gemsbok for me.'
He slept. The little dog watched him with its yellow eyes.
They were all lying down in the house.

The little dog crouched ready to spring at them,
and he startled awake, scolding it into submission. The woman,
sleepless, kept her son beside her,

pinching him to keep him awake,
keeping the baby tucked under her arm.
The young lion rose, moved away a little, sat upright, lay down.

The man arose, his wife after him. When he'd made up the fire
he slung his quiver over his shoulder, took the knobkerrie
and called the dog's name. The dog went trotting behind.

His wife said again to her child, 'The young lion goes yonder.
Don't imagine it's tame – it's wild and fierce, smelling our scent. It knows itself
a thing of the night. It kills people and eats them.'

The young lion crept up on her husband in the bush.
He turned on it, furious. It cowered, retreated. Effortless,
it killed a young gemsbok.

The man dashed up to the young lion
and it wheeled towards him, confronting. He bellowed –
it cantered back, growled at him, lay down.

The man, trembling, reached the young gemsbok,
dragged it under a Khui tree as the lion glared at him.
He scolded it, and called its new dog-name.

A name is a thing of power. The man gave the young lion
the name of a dog, thinking by naming it, he could control it,
could change its nature. But the young lion was born

with its own true name. '!Kuisse !khui/ku' the man called it, trying
to entice it. It listened, gazing at one who'd stolen it as a cub
from its mother – a long strange look.

The man laid down bushes on the ground and cut up the gemsbok.
He threw the lion lung meat which it caught mid-air and swallowed
with one gulp. He cut out the heart

and offered it: 'Here, !Kuisse !khui/ku.' The young lion
caught the gemsbok-heart in its jaws, and with it the man's hand.
He snatched his hand from the lion's jaws just in time.

He cut off the neck and flung it '!Kuisse !khui/ku here!'
Again the young lion nearly bit off his hand. The poor man
sprang away in fright, grabbed his stick, threatening

as the lion bound away with the young gemsbok's neck in his jaws.
The man's thinking strings were sounding:
I've broiled none of the gemsbok's meat for myself.

My dog's look is an ugly look. Perhaps I should make my escape
while the sun is still up so my dog can't surprise me,
get home, before it drags me down into darkness.

He prepared his load quick as he could, threading his arms into skin
of the gemsbok's feet, hoisting it up, watching the lion
with a nervous eye. He called it by its dog's name

glancing back fearfully as it trotted behind him.
One leg running, one limping, slipping his feet awkwardly
along the ground, he made his way homeward. His load was heavy.

The dog followed.
He held his stick high, ready to beat it back.
As he neared his house he called out to his wife, 'Get up! Quickly!'

His wife and child saw him approaching with the lion and quickly laid
wood on the fire. They piled up fire-sticks to hurl at the lion
as it approached with the man. They prepared hot coals.

The lion came galloping towards them. Its face was yellow.
The little boy cried to his mother, 'Wrap the baby on your back for safety!
I'll stand at the door, so it sees me first. You stand ready to shovel fire!'

The lion reached them. They hurled the fire-sticks and hot coals
again and again till they drove it back,
till it lay down in the shade, growling.

The man reached home,
still protesting that the lion was a dog his brother gave him,
confessed his terror to his wife.

She was not sympathetic. 'Your madness and lies will cost me a child!
I'm the one who has to lie watching at night while it watches us hungrily.
You're the one who comes deceiving us. You're the one who stole a lion cub

from its lioness mother!   You've not seen my brother-in-law at all.
He's with his father. You're a liar and a cheat!
You want to force me to accept a lie that will destroy us.'

The lion perked up, looking at her,
hearing its true name. 'My mother hush!' whispered the child.
'The dog is staring at you, listening to its name.'

She turned on her son: 'Are you blind! You still call this thing
a dog? This is the dog your father has fed, that will kill him.
What have his thinking strings done?'

* * * * * * *

And so the story goes on. And on and on.
We are living it now. The man took the young lion hunting again
till the lion killed him and ate him. His little son saw it all
and bore the news to his mother.

She took her children, and fled to her father-in-law's house. In time
her brother-in-law and her son returned to find the house destroyed
and the spoor of seven lions around it.
O deceitful hunter, nothing has changed.

All the clan moved to a far away place, leaving their homes
to escape a danger let loose, that could never be cured
for the lions, those things of the night, knew them, and would not forget.
And this is how we live.

[This narrative poem is created from the literal translation made by Lucy
Lloyd in 1873. She recorded an epic narrative given to her by ||Kabbo, which
she entitled: *The First /Xam Man Brings Home a Young Lion.* My version
is a re-working of only the first 79 manuscript pages of 553 manuscript
pages, with my last three stanzas a summary of the remainder of the story.
I've used the short line, and some poetic license, to remain as close as I could
to the original text, while attempting to capture the vividness and spirit of
the original.]

THE FIRST /XAM MAN BRINGS HOME
A YOUNG LION

This ancient story is startlingly contemporary in its message. Myths, like dreams, give us access to the unconscious, both individual and collective, and although the /Xam narrator, ||Kabbo, had no idea of the dangers that would be facing the world in 2016, he lived in a world that was systematically exterminating his people, and it would be absurd to imagine that he told it as a simple cautionary tale about a foolish hunter and the danger of lions. He was a Rainmaker and shape shifter. He was also a talented story teller able to leap with his mind across alien culture from the other side of the world, in order to make his stories understood. The issues the story raises were as relevant then as they are now: *We need to understand and respect our place in the order of nature.*

The hunter knows that the young lion will be useful to him in catching game. He also knows that lions are dangerous to people, but he persuades himself that in this case, through his good management in starting with such a young lion, all will be well. The speed, endurance, skill, and good luck necessary for a man to kill an antelope is considerable. The lion-hunter would be a good short cut, if it could be made to work for him. He wants flesh, and for him and his family, although roots are an edible diet, flesh is better. This is an ancient tradition. In the old testament story of Cain and Abel, the brother who offers God flesh is preferred to the brother who offers him corn.

For us, in the contemporary world, the need for *easy flesh* associated with damage to the natural order of nature can be compared to many dangerous wants we have to make our lives pleasanter. As collective humanity, we know how the way we use resources brings great danger into our collective lives, but like the First /Xam man, we want the results and don't want to face the associated implications.

A lion is the embodiment of all that is powerful, fierce, dangerous, impossible to control. In its place, the lion should be feared and respected, as well as honoured as pure power. In the /Xam world, Shamans both good and evil would sometimes take the form of lions to cross between planes of existence. Where the protagonist here goes wrong is in thinking he can harness the lion's power for his own benefit. He brings the lion cub into his home as a pet and a servant. This can only be inflation. He has lost all sense of himself in the order of nature. He massively overestimates his own power, and underestimates the power of the lion. For lion we could read "nuclear power", "genetic modification of seeds", "the hunger for oil" – and all the elements of inflation in our society that pose threats to our survival. When the baby lion grows up, we have nuclear disasters, devastating oil spills, climate change.

In the individual psyche in the grip of wanting something, there is the "hunter" part of us, that allows us to rationalise and distort our perception in order to conform with what we want. There is also the helpless "hunter's wife" aspect, that is not persuaded but cannot prevail. Thirdly, there is the naïve "child" aspect that is genuinely confused. And finally there is the "lion" aspect – the instinctual, ruthless, and hugely powerful elemental aspect that cannot be controlled. This scenario is always one of conflict and endless repetition in a disturbed mind.

In the political world ‖Kabbo found himself, it represents society in turmoil. It is also a familiar pattern in families. In Nieu Bethesda, for "lion" we easily substitute "alcohol" or "aids". The individual alcoholic thinks himself able to control the "lion" alcohol, and brings it into his home to make his life pleasanter. Doing so, he endangers his family as well as his own life. Very soon the alcohol controls him, taking away all peace and harmony from his home. His wife becomes a drunk like him. Alcohol uses up all their money. Family life consists of knife fights, screaming, fear. Love goes out of the window, proper work is no longer possible. Health breaks down. His children live in terror until they are old enough to drink themselves, and the whole cycle begins again.

In the /Xam story, the man brings danger into the house and his wife understand immediately. She does her best to dissuade him, but he will not

74

listen. He sticks to his story that the lion really is a dog who presents no danger. She knows he is lying and he knows that she knows, but will not concede. Instead he goes on the offensive, accusing her of insulting his brother. This sounds so much like the lies we are collectively forced to listen to again and again – about how safe and beneficial certain scientific or money-making schemes are for society at large. We are collectively patronised with the same superior attitude by those with power as the man displays to his wife.

The disaster, when it finally overtakes him, overtakes the whole family. One little lion cub becomes seven grown up lions, following his spoor, and threatening to annihilate the whole clan, who must find another place altogether to live. In these times of uncertainty about the survival of life on earth, this story is menacing and prophetic in a deeply disturbing way.

At the Arts Centre, we've performed this story as a play, as a shadow-puppet performance, and most recently, with giant puppets each controlled by four or five puppeteers. The themes that it explores – the tradition of naming, the theme of lies and truth – the difficulty for a child in disbelieving its parents, or for one parent in counteracting the lies of a deceitful other, the theme of self-deceit, of the abuse of power, and of spoiling one's environment till it is no longer possible to live there – all these are themes that make it a rich contribution to our contemporary culture, which is where it deserves a place.

|Kaggen, Red Hartebeest, !Gaunu-tsaxau, and the Baboons

|Kaggen, the Mantis, is a celestial trickster figure in /Xam mythology.

In the first of two stories depicted on this tapestry, |Kaggen takes the form of a red hartebeest, and lies down, pretending to be dead. Excited children find him and cut him up for food. The hartebeest head, carried by the smallest child, winks at her. It whispers: *"Loose the thong from my eye so I can see where we're going."* In terror she drops it on the ground. *Oh my poor head, oh bad little person*, says the dead hartebeest. The children flee in terror. The dismembered body resurrects and transforms into an old man, chasing them all the way home.

In the second story, |Kaggen's son, !Gaunu-tsaxau, (eye of !Gaunu, the Great Star) goes among the baboons to gather sticks for his father. The baboons first mock, and then kill him, and play ball with his eye. At noon |Kaggen, realising his son should have been home by now, goes in search of him, and finds the baboons in their monstrous game. He pretends to play with them, throws the eye into the sky, then hides it in his bag. The baboons give him a thorough beating before he flies away, and puts the eye into the spring where it grows again into his living child.

|Kaggen Assumes the Form of a Hartebeest

Narrated by ||Kabbo

Feigning death, |Kaggen, the Mantis, lay stretched out
horns backward, in the form of a dead hartebeest.
The children who found him jumped for joy.

'Our hartebeest! We shall eat great meat!'
They struck stones to make knives
skinned the hartebeest.

'Hold strongly fast for me
the hartebeest skin!' cried one. Another child puzzled:
'The hartebeest skin pulled at me!'

Her elder sister was also puzzled. 'The hartebeest seems
to have no shooting wound, and it's fat. It seems
to have died of itself.'

She cut off a shoulder, that elder sister,
put it down on a bush. The shoulder arose
and settled itself on the shadier side.

She cut off a thigh, put it down on a bush.
The thigh arose and settled itself more comfortably.
She cut off another shoulder and put it on a bush.

The shoulder arose. The bush where the child had laid it
felt prickly. It found a soft place on the bush
to sit on nice and comfy.

Another elder sister cut off another thigh.
They whispered, 'This hartebeest's flesh moves!
It shrinks away, like the flesh of a wounded man!'

but they didn't stop. They arranged their burdens
bossing each other: 'Cut and break off the hartebeest's neck
so the little sister can carry the head.'

'Big sister loafing over there – she can carry
the hartebeest's back.'... 'We need to get home!'
'Our hartebeest's flesh moves,

makes itself comfortable, snatches itself
out of our hands!'.... 'It's creepy!'.... 'Hurry up! Hurry!'
They mount the hartebeest's head on the little sister.

The head is heavy. They help her stand up, encouraging her:
'Father will roast it for you when we get home.'
Little sister struggled along behind her big sisters.

The head kept slipping, wriggling, loosed the thong from its eye.
It whispered to the child, 'O child, move the thong from my eye
so I can see where we're going.'

She turned to look and it winked at her.
She whimpered with fear. 'Come on, hurry up,' called her bossy sister.
'We have to get home!'

'But,' cried the child, 'this head can speak. It winked at me.
It asked me to take away the thong from its eye.'
Big sister was scathing: 'Don't be an idiot! Heads don't speak.'

Little sister peeped round again. Open. Closed. Open. Closed.
'It's alive!' she yelled. 'It keeps opening and closing its eyes!'
She dropped it on the ground.

'O my head,' scolded |Kaggen. 'O bad little person,
hurting my poor head!'
Her sisters let fall the flesh of |Kaggen and fled.

Severed head, neck, spine, back, thigh, chest, shoulder blade, ribs
leapt in the air, raced over the ground, sprang forward
towards each other and joined, joined, joined together.

In the form of a man he pursued the children, shoulders jogging,
shoes on his feet, till they reached their home. Then quickly
he jogged along the river bed and came up on the other side of the hill

near his home. Breathless, babbling, the children poured out their story.
'We found a dead hartebeest and cut it up to bring home.'
'The flesh quivered, snatched itself from our hands,

made itself comfy on the bushes.'
'The head whispered to our little sister.'… 'Papa,' said the little girl,
'do you believe me? It *did* speak. It stared at my neck. It told me to remove

the thong from its eye!' Her father said,
'Have you been and cut up the old man, ǀKaggen,
while he lay pretending to be dead in front of you?'

Out came the story again, horns, hair, no arrow wound,
a talking head. Flesh that leaps in the air and springs together, gathers itself
whole, mends itself. A hartebeest that is red, swinging its arms like a man,

a thing pursuing them, running before the wind,
sun lighting up the soles of its shoes,
disappears into the river bed, and comes up behind the hill.

'You are those who went and cut up the old man,
Old Tinderbox Owner,' said the parents. 'He was the one who gently
slipped out from the place of hiding.'

'We ran as fast as we could but he always seemed in front of us.
We laid our karosses on our shoulders and ran faster.'
'That hartebeest head talked to our poor little sister.'

'His arms were waving fast as he chased us. We were so tired,
our hearts were burning. He deceived us. He wanted to cheat us,
pretending to be dead, pretending to be a hartebeest.'

'He scared us on purpose, in front of all the people.'
'He pretended he was gathering wood in the little river bed
while we came carrying his thighs. He talked while his flesh

mended itself. He's a deceiver. He made us tired on purpose.'
'From now on we'll not go hunting for food.'
'From now on we will altogether remain at home.'

|Kaggen, !Gaunu-tsaxau and the Baboons

Narrated by |han‡kass'õ, 1878, who heard it from his mother, |xabbi-an.

A stick for an arrow is quite particular
straight and true, without duplicity. Long ago !Gaunu-tsaxau,
the son of |Kaggen

went among the baboons to find sticks for his father.
The baboons were feeding round and about.
An old baboon confronted him, firing questions.

Politely the child answered:
'I must fetch sticks for my father,
that he might take aim at the people who sit on their heels.'

'Hie!' exclaimed the baboon, 'Come listen to this child!'
(He spoke in Baboon language which is not easy
so I tell it in my own language.) The other replied:

First going
I listen
to the child yonder!
First going
I listen
to the child yonder!

The baboons came loping up from far and wide, going, coming,
muddled together. 'Listen to this child! Hie! Come hear this child!'
They called to each other to come and listen.

First going
I listen
to the child yonder.

They made him repeat his story. Guffawing, they chanted
to each other: 'He means us!' The old men baboons gathered around
jeering, mocking: 'Oho, it is ourselves he means to shoot.'

All shouting at once: 'Listen to this child!
He wants to fetch sticks for his father to take aim
at the people who sit on their heels. It is we ourselves he means!'

Their eyes darkened. 'Strike the child with your fists!'
In a mob they beat the child, broke open his head,
knocked out his eye while he lay dying.

And I want it.
Whose ball is it?
And I want it.
Whose ball is it?
And I want it.
My companion's ball it is.
And I want it.
My companion's ball.
And I want it.
My ball,
my ball it is
and I want it.
My companion's ball it is,
and I want it.
My companion's ball,
and I want it.

They chanted, played a ball-game with the child's eye.
As noon blazed |Kaggen
getting fearful for his son, who had not come home

laid himself down and entered, as he often did,
his seeing dream. Here time and the bush melted
to a diffrent way of seeing and he saw it all clearly,

how they killed the child and played ball with his eye.
Oh !Gaunu-tsaxau, my son! |Kaggen had an old brave song:
Rattling along, rattling along. He sang courage to himself

as he slung on his quiver with its rattling arrows,
and came to the baboon's dust
where they were playing ball with his little son's eye.

Secretly he cried,
he cried, he cried, then dried his tears and hid his sadness.
He ran up to the baboons, startling them, and they stared.

'Why are you staring?' he shouted, and grabbed at the ball.
They flung it over his head but he grabbed it. 'Let me play too!'
The eye caught the scent of its father and |Kaggen

anointed it with his sweat, then hurled it up up up – as star
it ascended into the sky, as eye came down by |Kaggen's quiver.
The baboons gawped, watching it cut an arc into the blue

could not follow, wanted it, wanted it, did not understand
what they were wanting. It seemed the eye leapt over the bag
but really was hiding inside it.

The baboons looked everywhere for the eye.
'Where's our ball? Give me the ball!' |Kaggen pretended to look as well.
'Where's the ball? Where's your ball?'

'Shake out your bag,' roared the baboons.
'It's in your bag.' |Kaggen grasped the eye and turned the bag
inside out. 'See, it's not here. The bag's empty!

I haven't got your ball.'
'Hit the old man with your fists,' exclaimed a baboon.
'Give us our ball!' yelled the baboon, striking |Kaggen's head.

'I haven't got your ball,' said |Kaggen, striking the baboon's head.
They were all striking |Kaggen's head with their fists,
he striking them too, but getting the worst of it.

Ow! ow! cried |Kaggen. *Hartebeest's children,* (meaning his bag which,
like all his things, was alive) *you must go! !kau !Yerriggu! You must go!*
The bag flew up into the air, and he with it, shouting:

I !ke. tten !khwaiten! khwaiten, !kui ha I !ka! He flew to the water
and dived in, came out of the water, holding his bag,
took the child's eye and sat in the grass on the bank of the pool.

He made a spell: *Oh wwi ho!* and gently slipped the child's eye
into the green water: *Thou must grow, grow, grow and become*
that which thou hast been. Sadly, he slung his kaross

over his shoulder, slung on his quiver, made his way home.
The Ichneumon was indignant: 'Who's done this to my grandfather?
He's covered in wounds!'... 'The baboons,' replied |Kaggen.

'They caught our !Gaunu-tsaxau, killed him, played ball with his eye.
They accused me of taking their ball, and fought me.
So I fought them, then flying came home.'

The rest of the story he didn't tell –
how he'd put the child's eye
into the water.

|kuamman-a was surly: 'Ask Grandfather why he continually goes
amongst people who are different!' |Kaggen answered, 'Can't you see?
It was yearning that made me go among the baboons.'

He waited as long as he could, then returned to the pool. Gently
he crept up, quietly, closer,
but the child heard him far off, and splashed away

into the water. He laughed with joy, yearning for the child,
returned home, altogether returned, and waited.
The child grew, till it was like that which it had formerly been.

|Kaggen returned, creeping, straining to see his child,
spied him sitting in the sun
but the child heard rustling in the grass and still a wild thing

sprang up and away into the water. |Kaggen stood,
gazed long and deep into the pool, searching for a glimpse of his face
had at last to drag himself away.

Then he made clothes for the child, a kaross, a ||koroko.
He crept gently to the rock where the child lay in the sun,
opposite the water. Hearing him, the child was ready to spring away

but quick as a dragonfly |Kaggen caught hold of him.
He anointed the child with his scent. He said,
Why art thou afraid of me, I am thy father.

I who am |Kaggen, I am here.
Thou art my son, thou art !Gaunu-tsaxau,
I am |Kaggen, I whose son thou art, thy father is myself.

So the child sat down, tamed, and his father dressed him:
Front kaross, ||koroko, gently he dressed him. Frail as a sprite,
the child went with |Kaggen, returned to his home,

where the Ichneumon made a row: 'Now who is this
you're bringing home? Why did you tell us the child was dead,
yet you bring him home? Killed by the baboons, you said!'

|Kaggen explained to his grandson
who only ever saw the appearance of things:
'Baboons are like noise in your head.

Don't you see that the child's not strong? I didn't know
if that I wished for could accomplish itself for me.
He feels that I put his eye into the pool to regenerate,

took time, came out of the water. I needed to wait,
taking care of him. I needed patience, waiting and caring
to see if he'd become strong.'

|KAGGEN, RED HARTEBEEST, !GAUNU-TSAXAU, AND THE BABOONS

There are two stories depicted in one tapestry. The first is the story of the Mantis trickster |Kaggen taking the form of a red hartebeest. The second much more complex and disturbing, is his encounter with the baboons. The former presents the trickster motif at its simplest. For no apparent reason, Mantis tricks the children into thinking he is a dead hartebeest, allows them to cut him up, and then scares them almost to death as they try to carry him home. Who is this wily old man? Why should he do this to the children? Underneath the mischief and humour of the story, there is a clear lesson for the children: *Things are not what they seem. All nature is alive, and should be treated with respect. You are foolish children if you think you can go out and cut up whatever you want.*

As a fairy-tale might work in the western cannon, in this story it's when the grown-ups are absent that the children have an adventure, and get into trouble. Within this structure the Mantis becomes the dangerous ogre in the forest. Here, though, the children don't in any way outwit him as they would in a European counterpart. They simply flee, and remain in a state of terror till they reach the safety of their parents' home. Of all the stories Lucy Lloyd transcribed, this was the one she chose to begin with in her book, *Specimens of Bushmen Folklore*. Perhaps because it's funny, she considered it the most accessible and attractive of the stories for her Western readers. More importantly, she was marking out the territory. This creature, the Mantis, is implicit at the centre of all the stories, and must be taken into account, even though he is beyond rational comprehension.

Seen as an intra-psychic adventure, the psyche here is divided into three fundamental elements: the gullible, immature self, governed by the senses, and represented here by the children; the wiser, experienced ego-consciousness represented by the parents, and then the incomprehensible, erratic, irrational, and frighteningly powerful element which we call the unconscious. Understood in this way, the story is an introduction to the mythology of the /Xam, a gateway that entices you in with a first taste of what is to come.

The trickster figure in /Xam mythology is an archetype for the unconscious, which is paradoxical, dangerous, creative, mischievous. It's forever elusive, yet when it intervenes, there's no mistaking its presence. All our tapestries have several small Mantises perched in them somewhere, but I avoided working with the Trickster directly in our tapestries for years, daunted by its complexity, and afraid of unleashing the inherent darkness contained within the archetype. With hindsight, this is a big joke, as the

Trickster was omnipresent in all my work in Nieu Bethesda, and as ubiquitous as our little hidden Mantises. When we finally started making our first large Mantis tapestry, the archetypal Trickster was unleashed in full force. One huge and amazing piece of work caused such havoc among our artists we decided to scrap it. Another was pure shadow. A third is probably our best tapestry to date.

As a psychotherapist, the focus of my work has been to do with the unconscious, and the shadow side of human beings. Within this shifting space the trickster squats. |Kaggen, called the Mantis by Lloyd, is amoral, deceitful, resourceful. Like the magical creatures of dreams, he can transform into many different forms; like the insect whose name he bears, he is hard to spot, but lightning fast in the kill, and imitating the insect Mantis, who grows wings quite late in its life cycle, |Kaggen can suddenly sprout wings to escape from an enemy. True to the unconscious we all meet every day, he carries pain, he bears grudges and he dreams the world into being. He is cunning, foolish, passionate in his loving, quarrelsome, at times beaten and humiliated, but one who rises triumphant out of death again and again. He contains the dualism and paradox of humanity itself. We could say of |Kaggen that he represents the essence, the spirit of our species. All other characters in the stories are limited and one-dimensional beside him. It is almost as if the stories are built around him, to display his many aspects – like walking into a hall of mirrors to see ourselves reflected in our many forms.

The trickster is the creative principle. In the /Xam mythology he is the one who collects honey from the bush. Honey is an archetype for universal sweetness, product of the bees, fertilisers of all life. He is the creator of the Eland, the largest antelope in the landscape, symbolising the bounty of nature. The red hartebeest, another large antelope and source of bounty for the /Xam, is his creature. He's a shape-shifter, as the creative principle must always be. He rises from the fire, a new creature. He is full of surprises, outrageous as the artist should be.

He is argumentative, at times unwisely brave in challenging the majority, without calculating the odds of getting hurt. As artists often do, he challenges the power base, gets beaten up, and then transcends his persecutors. (I think of those persecuted Russian poets whose poems were whispered from prisoner to prisoner in Siberia, kept alive till it was safe for them to be written down.)

Following Lloyd's selection, we chose the same two stories when we finally began our work of exploring the huge theme of the trickster. Skotnes also chooses one of them to begin her monumental book on the archive, *Claim to the Country*.

Skotnes imagines how difficult it must have been for |han‡kass'õ to patiently tell Lucy Lloyd in her leafy home in Mowbray the story of |Kaggen

who went among people who were different – the baboons who had killed his son – while Ihan‡kass'õ himself was among people who were different: *"the policeman who beat his wife to death, the Dutch farmers who were looting his honey hives and occupying his land, the herders whose animals were drinking at his waterholes and the British officials who had first captured him, set him in stocks, and then made him roll stones for a break-water that was to be named after the Queen of England . . ."*

Skotnes then considers how the words "people who are different" (!k'e e /xarra) was culled from the archive and optimistically used to make the phrase "!k'e e /xarra //ke" (people who are different come together) – now the new democracy's motto and the wording on South Africa's coat of arms.

For us in Nieu Bethesda, a rather more inward relationship with the story emerged. I was working with people who, as descendants of the original informants, were at the end of a time-line of persecution and degradation that had lasted for centuries. Now they were on the very brink of survival. My concern, though the external realities of racial prejudice, poverty and social ills were constantly addressed, was focussed on inner transformation. My interest is in directing understanding into the dark places in the psyche.

Baboons, and !Gaunu-tsaxau, Mantis's beloved son, can both be read as aspects of the Mantis's psyche. !Gaunu-tsaxau is the immature ego, that is guileless, truthful, fragile. The baboons, whom Mantis wants to make war on, are his "lower self" instinctual, dangerous when aroused. Part of that instinctual nature is what we sometimes call "the monkey mind" – the endless chattering of useless thoughts.

If we were to try to think of an image for the persistent, cunning, jabbering thoughts that occupy our minds most of the time, it would be difficult to think of a more apt image than these ruthless old baboons. When we try to still them, "make war on" these thoughts, we project at first a naïve and vulnerable part of ourselves among them. The baboons easily kill off that intention, and play havoc with our perception – imaged in this story by the baboons playing ball with !Gaunu-tsaxau's eye.

The Mantis sends the immature ego to gather wood for arrows to make war on his monkey mind – a doomed enterprise from the beginning. "It is as hard to control the mind as to still the wind" says Arjuna in the Bhagavad Gita.[1] Of course the small and helpless child falls victim to the troupe of large, jabbering baboons. It is not until noon when consciousness (the sun) is at its highest, that ǀKaggen realises something has gone wrong. Through his love, cunning, patience, bravery and magical powers, the Mantis is able to save his son's "eye" (in other words, his own true perception). Through the life-giving power of water, and using the magical technique of fractal regeneration (the whole reflected in a part), he is able to renew and restore his untainted perception of the world.

The cost of this venture is high. Both physically and emotionally ǀKaggen

1. The Bhagavad Gita, 1967, P.395/34

gets a beating. Innocence is no match for the monkey mind. The power of baboons should not be underestimated, and the mature and resolute ego is needed to get the better of them.

|Kaggen is the only character in these stories I have come across who carries a bag, and he is seldom without it. The bag is the tool-bag the Self carries on its journey. The bag represents that organ of connectedness in us that makes it possible to live a guided life. It is only by using his bag, a magical object that speaks, understands and always responds to him, that he is able to retrieve the eye, and make his escape.

|Kaggen's encounter with the baboons is a transformative story. He is not the same as he was. His innocent and naïve self dies, the perception (eye) of that naïve self is elevated, (thrown up into the sky) and then plunged into a pool (life force) where it regenerates. The Ichneumon (|Kaggen's grandson) does not recognise the risen !Gaunu-tsaxsau, because that Ichneumon part of the psyche does not recognise a higher form of perception. There is always a part of us that does not want to grow, and always chooses to stick to the

old ways and known people. |kwamann-a, his son in law, says exasperated, "Ask grandfather why he continually goes among people who are different". |Kaggen answers with what is perhaps the most important sentence in these stories: "Can't you see it was yearning that made me go among the baboons."

> *I needed to wait,*
> *taking care of him. I needed patience, waiting and caring*
> *to see if he'd become strong.*

In the final part of this story, |Kaggen enters a kind of dance of patience and alertness. He has to temper his joy that the child is alive with utmost patience and alertness, or it will elude him. This is the dance of the seeker who yearns for union with his or her soul. The joy of that union must be contained, held in consciousness, and sought with patience and continuous remembrance, until the time comes that it can be tamed.

> *"I am |Kaggen, I whose son thou art, thy father is myself."*

The Origin of Darkness and of the Moon

The Mantis, whose name was |Kaggen, created from his son-in-law's shoe a tiny live eland. He did this by putting the shoe into a sacred pool, surrounded by reeds. Each day he would go into the bush, and find honey for his eland. He would place it in a hollow rock near the pool, and hiding in the reeds, watch, joyfully, as the tiny eland ate it.

The eland thrived and grew until it was the biggest and most beautiful of all Africa's antelope. Whenever he looked at it, |Kaggen's heart swelled with love.

Meanwhile the meerkats were angry that |Kaggen was no longer bringing them honey. They set his grandson, the Ichneumon, to spy on him. The Ichneumon, hiding in |Kaggen's bag, slit a hole in the bag and spied the eland in all its glory. As soon as he could, the Ichneumon rushed to the meerkats, and told them about the eland, and immediately they slaughtered it.

|Kaggen, out in the bush gathering honey as usual for his eland, found the honey not fat, but dry, and at once he knew something was wrong. He hurried to the pool, and called his eland, but the eland didn't come. Instead he found blood on the hollow rock where he usually gave the eland honey.

His heart breaking, |Kaggen followed the trail of blood to where he found the meerkats feasting on the eland they'd slain. In a fury he pulled out his arrows and took aim. But because the meerkats had killed the eland, the fight-power of the great animal went into them, so |Kaggen's arrows turned around and went straight back to him. Desperate, he grabbed his knob-kerrie and rushed into the thick of them, but they easily took the knob-kerrie, and beat him to within inches of his life. To humiliate him even further, they forced him to gather wood for their fires where they were roasting the eland flesh.

Broken, wounded, full of pain |Kaggen crept away. On a bush he found the gall bladder of his slaughtered eland, where the meerkats had set it aside. In his grief he cut the gall bladder open, and darkness poured out, enveloping the earth. Then he threw his shoe up into the sky, where it became the moon, so there was light enough for him to take flight.

The Origin of Darkness and of the Moon

Narrated 1873/74, by Diä!kwãin, who had it from his mother

A shoe is a thing of power. ǀKaggen, the Mantis
dipped in a sacred pool the Rainbow's shoe
and from that meeting – earth, light, water

he created a tiny live Eland. Neat as a seed
perfectly formed, eyes open, horns turned back
hooves folded together and live heart beating

it nestled in his green hand. ǀKaggen gazed at it
in awe. In the reeds by the pool
he kept it hidden from all eyes but his own.

ǀKaggen, transformer, master of honey
went humming to the bees as he always did,
gathered for his new creature

honey that was fat. It was rich, it was molten
sunlight. Bag brimming
he poured into a hollowed-out stone that

gold that sweetens the tongue
and the Eland ate its fill, thrived and grew till
it was biggest, most beautiful of all antelope.

ǀKaggen loved his creation.
'Where's our honey?' raged his Meerkat relations.
'Honey's lean in the bush today,' he lied calmly.

What he did with his honey was his business.
Meerkats standing upright act like miniature
humans and like humans, they're devious.

The Meerkat family felt cheated, entitled,
groomed the young Ichneumon,
|Kaggen's grandson, to spy.

'Grandfather, take me into the bush with you
to gather honey,' pleaded the young Ichneumon.
So |Kaggen hauled him along in a sack.

'Take a sharp stone in your mouth, to cut a peep-hole,'
the Meerkat brothers whispered so young Ichneumon
spied through a peephole the Eland in its glory.

'Tonight I will sleep with my brothers.'
'Come sleep with grandfather as usual' said |Kaggen
but the child shifted, avoided his eye.

Next day in the bush the smell of the wind, birdsong,
muscles under his skin, the bush itself felt stiff with betrayal
and the honey was dry in the rustling bush.

|Kaggen rushed to the water hole, called into the reeds
his special call: *Come out, my beauty.*
Silence. Too late.

The Ichneumon had taken the Meerkats
straight to the Eland's pool, shown them how to call it
out of hiding with /Kaggen's call. Slain it.

Blood on the hollowed stone.
In his pain |Kaggen followed the blood trail to
Meerkats in a mob, slicing, skinning, feasting.

Greasy smoke. Smell of roast flesh. Laughter.
He grabbed his bow and quiver
but the Eland's fight was in his arrows –

mid-air the arrows turned and attacked him.
His own knobkerrie rained blows onto his body
and the Meerkats beat him to the edge of his life.

'Go fetch wood for our fires, old man!' they jeered
sent him creeping away into the scrub
heavy with wounds. Weeping, groping for wood

he found the gall-bladder of his Eland slung on a bush.
His grief pierced it open and darkness poured out
filled the world, turning it black.

In the first terrible darkness of the world
|Kaggen took off his shoe and hurled it into the sky.
A shoe is a thing of power.

Up up up it climbed, getting brighter each moment
till it became the moon. |Kaggen, that shape-shifter,
opened wings and flew away home.

Some say this slaughter for food was the first on earth
and the herds of antelope that enrich our land
sprang from drops of the Eland's blood.

THE ORIGIN OF DARKNESS AND OF THE MOON

This complex myth is my favourite of the Trickster stories. It begins with ǀKaggen gathering honey. When the meerkats kill the sacred Eland, the honey in the bush goes dry. The consequences are unstoppable – darkness is unleashed on the world. This is a poignant and frighteningly contemporary symbol for our world now, where the bees are actually threatened.

When ǀKaggen decides to use the honey he normally gathers to feed his eland, his family are angry. They betray him, destroying the best part of him. This is exactly what happens in the psyche. Deprived of dreams, deprived of its creativity, the mind becomes monstrous, turning traitor to its human host. The trail of blood, the meerkats feasting around their fires, ǀKaggen being denigrated and humiliated in their service, represents the human being at his lowest, in a state of breakdown. The scene also works at the level of a social collapse, where society has destroyed the best of its values.

ǀKaggen's family appear as characters in most of his adventures. They behave like normal families, and give him a very human aspect. But we should also read them as part of the intra-psychic three dimensional dance of aspects of the Great Trickster.

ǀKaggen has a strong feminine side, and in his family he is surrounded by females. His wife is Dassie. Dassie is fat, delicious. Dassie is without harm – eats only grass, is shy when threatened, serene when safe. There is no aggression in her. In fact she is the counterpart of aggression. When our artists see a dassie, their mouths water. His sister is the blue crane, most beautiful of all South African birds. He also has an adopted daughter, Xo, the porcupine. Porcupine, our artists agree, is the most delicious of all wild meat, and on one porcupine, there is a great deal of fat. It is hard to get at because of all the porcupine quills. And Xo's father is the Bushfire. You feel him. You run from him. His shadow is smoke, and there is no escaping him when he surrounds you. Xo is well protected. She contains the dark side of the feminine that is not to be messed with.

He has two sons. One of his sons is Little Mantis. The other is a star, !Gaunu's eye. Gaunu is the great star, who sang all the other stars into being, and named them. !Gaunu-tsaxau is of course to do with perception. He is the young, and developing part of ǀKaggen's psyche. He is most precious. Xo's husband is ǀkuamman-a. He is in the Rainbow, and sometimes he *is* the Rainbow. He is important in the story of the Origin of Darkness and the Moon, because it is from his shoe that ǀKaggen creates the sacred Eland. The Rainbow is seen as magical, special, in most cultures. Where the rainbow

touches the earth is a magical space. The point at which the rainbow touches the earth is the shoe of |kuamman-a – but |Kaggen has to steal it to create the Eland. This precious, creative, magical space in all of us is not always easy to access. |kuamman-a never addresses |Kaggen directly. |Kaggen's grandson is the Ichneumon, the always critical thorn in his flesh, the part of the self that obstinately refuses to grow. It is this part of his psyche that betrays him in this story.

When |Kaggen finds the gall-bladder of his eland tossed on a bush, his grief can no longer be contained. No bodily substance is as bitter as gall. His bitterness rips the gall-bladder open and darkness pours out over the earth. The whole scene is engulfed in darkness, until |Kaggen throws his shoe up into the sky. A shoe is a thing of power. It enables us to walk on stony ground. We become mobile, powerful, instead of helpless. His shoe in the sky becomes the moon, a source of light in the dark world. The moon is a celestial light, but unlike the sun, which represents consciousness, the moon represents the light of the imagination, that is born out of darkness.

References

The Bleek/Lloyd manuscripts written in the 19th century were rough translations in the form of notes in a number of notebooks, over a long period, by various narrators, written down by linguists Bleek and Lloyd. A small selection was published in 1911: *Specimens of Bushmen Folklore* – Lucy Lloyd and Wilhelm Bleek. The whole collection was published digitally by Pippa Skotnes in *Claim to the Country* – Pippa Skotnes, (2007). As they stand in the original manuscripts they cannot be coherently read. Many people have taken those notes and transcribed them into forms that can be read and understood. However every transcript is a matter of opinion, emphasis, preference, and choice of language. Some of these transcripts have been published as poems, for example *Return of the Moon* by Stephen Watson, (1991); *The First Bushman's Path* by Alan James, (2001); *The stars say 'tsau'* by Antjie Krog, (2004). Many have been published as prose, for example *Stories that Float from Afar* by J. D. Lewis-Williams, (2000). Some have been transcribed within academic articles and books, for example *Bushman Letters* by Michael Wessels, (2010), and *The Broken String* by Neil Bennun (2004). Inevitably, all reflect the bias of the writer, which is as it should be.

Jeni Couzyn and Toetie Dow, the senior traditional leader of the San people of the Eastern Cape. Photo courtesy of Eugene Coetzee, *The Herald.*